Unlocking Social Media Success: 30-Day Growth Hacks for Small Business Owners

Louise Gray

Table of contents

Introduction: Why Social Media Growth is Essential for Small Businesses

In today's digital age, social media has become an integral part of our daily lives. People all around the world use platforms like Facebook, Instagram, Twitter, and LinkedIn to connect with friends, family, and even brands. For small business owners, social media presents a unique opportunity to reach and engage with a larger audience, build brand awareness, and ultimately drive business growth.

This book "Unlocking Social Media Success: 30-Day Growth Hacks for Small Business Owners" is designed to provide small business owners with practical strategies and techniques to maximize their presence on social media platforms. Whether you are just starting out or looking to revamp your existing social media strategy, this book will guide you through a step-by-step process to achieve significant growth within a 30-day timeframe.

The importance of social media growth for small businesses cannot be overstated. It offers a cost-effective way to promote your products or services, establish your brand's authority, and foster meaningful connections with your target audience. Moreover, social media platforms provide valuable insights and analytics that can help you understand your audience better, refine your marketing strategies, and drive informed decision-making.

Throughout this book, you will learn how to set clear goals and objectives for your social media efforts, identify your target audience, craft a compelling brand story, and choose the right platforms to reach your target customers effectively. You will discover strategies to optimize your social media profiles, create engaging and shareable content, and implement a content calendar to maintain consistency and relevance.

Additionally, you will explore growth hacks such as leveraging the power of hashtags, engaging with your audience, collaborating with influencers and partners, and running contests and giveaways to boost engagement. You will also delve into advanced topics like utilizing social media advertising, harnessing the potential of video content, and monitoring social media analytics to measure the effectiveness of your efforts.

By the end of this 30-day journey, you will have gained the knowledge and tools necessary to build a lasting social media presence for your small business. So, let's dive in and unlock the immense potential of social media for your business growth!

Day 1: Setting Clear Goals and Objectives

Welcome to Day 1 of your 30-day journey towards social media growth for your small business! Today is all about setting clear goals and objectives for your social media strategy. Without a clear direction, it's challenging to measure your progress and determine whether your efforts are yielding the desired results.

Setting goals provides focus and helps you prioritize your social media activities. Start by asking yourself: What do I want to achieve through social media? Are you looking to increase brand awareness, generate leads, drive website traffic, boost sales, or enhance customer engagement? Each goal will require a different approach and set of strategies.

Once you have identified your primary goals, it's important to make them specific, measurable, attainable, relevant, and time-bound (SMART goals). For example, instead of saying, "I want to increase brand awareness," a SMART goal would be, "I want to increase brand awareness by 20% within the next three months through social media platforms."

Next, break down your main goals into smaller objectives that align with your overall business objectives. These objectives could include increasing your social media following, improving engagement rates, driving traffic to your website, or generating a certain number of leads or sales.

Remember to keep your goals and objectives realistic and aligned with your available resources. It's better to focus on a few key objectives that you can dedicate your time and effort to rather than spreading yourself too thin across multiple goals.

Once you have set your goals and objectives, write them down and refer to them regularly. This will keep you focused and motivated throughout your social media journey. Additionally, periodically review and reassess your goals to ensure they remain relevant and adjust them if necessary based on your progress and evolving business needs.

By setting clear goals and objectives, you lay the foundation for a successful social media strategy. With a well-defined direction, you can tailor your content, engagement tactics, and measurement techniques to achieve meaningful growth and measurable results.

Tomorrow, we will dive into Day 2: Identifying Your Target Audience. Stay tuned and get ready to discover the key to reaching the right people with your social media efforts.

Day 2: Identifying Your Target Audience

Welcome to Day 2 of your 30-day social media growth hack journey for small business owners! Today, we'll be focusing on a crucial aspect of your social media strategy: identifying your target audience. Understanding who your audience is and what they want is essential for creating relevant and engaging content that resonates with them.

To begin, take some time to research and analyze your existing customer base. Look at their demographics, such as age, gender, location, and income level. Identify common traits and characteristics among your customers to paint a clear picture of your target audience.

Next, delve deeper into their psychographics. Psychographics go beyond demographics and focus on attitudes, interests, values, and behaviors. Ask yourself questions like: What are their pain points and challenges? What motivates them? What are their interests and hobbies? What are their preferred social media platforms? Understanding these psychographic factors will help you craft content that speaks directly to your audience's needs and desires.

In addition to analyzing your current customer base, conduct market research to identify potential new target audiences. Look at industry trends, competitor analysis, and customer surveys to gain insights into untapped markets or segments that align with your product or service offering.

Once you have a clear understanding of your target audience, create buyer personas. These are fictional representations of your ideal customers, including their demographics, psychographics, goals, challenges, and buying behaviors. Developing buyer personas helps you humanize your audience, enabling you to tailor your messaging and content to their specific needs and preferences.

Remember that your target audience may evolve over time, so it's important to regularly reassess and refine your buyer personas based on new data and market trends.

By identifying your target audience, you can streamline your social media efforts and deliver content that speaks directly to the people who are most likely to engage with your brand. This targeted approach will not only increase engagement and conversions but also save you time and resources by avoiding irrelevant marketing efforts.

Tomorrow, on Day 3, we will explore the art of crafting a compelling brand story. Get ready to captivate your audience and differentiate your business from the competition.

Day 3: Crafting a Compelling Brand Story

Welcome to Day 3 of your 30-day social media growth hack journey for small business owners! Today, we'll be diving into the art of crafting a compelling brand story. A strong brand story is the foundation of your brand's identity and can deeply resonate with your target audience, forging a meaningful connection and setting you apart from the competition.

Your brand story is more than just a tagline or a mission statement. It's a narrative that encapsulates the essence of your brand, its values, and its unique selling proposition. It's the story of how your business came to be, what drives you, and why your audience should care.

To begin crafting your brand story, reflect on the roots of your business. What inspired you to start this venture? What problem were you trying to solve? Share the personal experiences or challenges that led you to where you are today. This humanizes your brand, making it relatable and fostering an emotional connection with your audience.

Next, highlight the values that guide your business. What principles and beliefs are at the core of your brand? Consider the impact you want to make in the lives of your customers and society as a whole. Your brand story should align with these values, showing your audience that you are more than just a profit-driven entity.

As you develop your brand story, think about how your product or service solves a problem or fulfills a need in your target audience's lives. What makes your offering unique and different from competitors? Communicate the benefits and value your brand provides, emphasizing how it improves the lives of your customers.

Remember to infuse your brand story with authenticity. Be genuine and transparent about who you are as a brand. Authenticity builds trust and fosters a stronger connection with your audience. Share real-life anecdotes, testimonials, or case studies that demonstrate the positive impact your brand has had on customers.

Visual elements can also play a significant role in conveying your brand story. Use compelling imagery, such as photographs or videos, that visually represent your brand's values and personality. Visual storytelling can captivate your audience's attention and create a lasting impression.

Once you have crafted your brand story, ensure consistency across all your social media platforms. Integrate your brand story into your bio, About Us sections, and posts. Use a consistent tone of voice that aligns with your brand's personality. This consistency will reinforce your brand's identity and make it instantly recognizable to your audience.

Your brand story should evolve over time as your business grows and adapts to changes.

Regularly revisit and refine your brand story to ensure it remains relevant and aligned with your current objectives and audience preferences.

Crafting a compelling brand story sets the stage for building a strong and lasting relationship with your audience. It creates a sense of loyalty and emotional connection that goes beyond the transactional nature of business. By telling your brand story effectively, you position your business as more than just a product or service—it becomes a part of your customers' lives.

Tomorrow, on Day 4, we will explore the process of choosing the right social media platforms for your business. Get ready to strategically select the platforms that will help you reach and engage with your target audience effectively.

Day 4: Choosing the Right Social Media Platforms for Your Business

Welcome to Day 4 of your 30-day social media growth hack journey for small business owners! Today, we'll be delving into the process of choosing the right social media platforms for your business. With so many platforms available, it's important to strategically select the ones that align with your target audience and business objectives.

To begin, conduct thorough research on the demographics and user behavior of different social media platforms. Each platform has its own unique user base and features, making it essential to understand which ones will provide the greatest opportunity for reaching your target audience.

Consider the age range, gender distribution, location, and interests of the users on each platform. For example, if your target audience consists mainly of young professionals, platforms like LinkedIn or Instagram may be more suitable. On the other hand, if you're targeting a younger demographic, platforms like TikTok or Snapchat may offer better engagement opportunities.

It's also crucial to consider the nature of your business and the type of content you want to share. Some platforms are more visually focused, such as Instagram and Pinterest, which are ideal for businesses in industries like fashion, food, or travel. If your business relies heavily on video content, platforms like YouTube or TikTok may be the best fit. Understanding the strengths and limitations of each platform will help you make an informed decision.

Additionally, evaluate the engagement and interaction levels on each platform. Some platforms prioritize user-generated content and community engagement, while others focus more on broadcasting and advertising. Choose platforms that align with your desired level of interaction and the type of engagement you want to foster with your audience.

Don't feel pressured to be present on every social media platform. It's better to have a strong presence on a few platforms than a mediocre presence on many. Focus your efforts on platforms that align most closely with your target audience and business objectives.

Once you have identified the platforms that are most relevant to your business, establish a consistent brand presence across them. Optimize your profiles with consistent branding elements, such as logos, color schemes, and taglines. Tailor your content strategy to the unique features and strengths of each platform, while maintaining a cohesive brand message.

Regularly monitor the performance and engagement levels on each platform. Analyze metrics such as reach, engagement, click-through rates, and conversions to assess the effectiveness of your presence on each platform. This data will guide your future decisions and allow you to allocate resources effectively.

Remember, the social media landscape is ever-evolving. Stay informed about emerging platforms and trends to evaluate their relevance to your business periodically. Experiment with new platforms if they align with your target audience and business objectives, but be prepared to adjust your strategy if they don't yield the desired results.

Choosing the right social media platforms for your business is a critical step in your social media growth journey. By focusing your efforts on platforms that resonate with your target audience and align with your business objectives, you maximize your chances of reaching and engaging with the right people in a meaningful way.

Tomorrow, on Day 5, we will explore the process of optimizing your social media profiles. Get ready to make a strong impression and effectively showcase your brand across various platforms.

Day 5: Optimizing Your Social Media Profiles

Welcome to Day 5 of your 30-day social media growth hack journey for small business owners! Today, we'll be focusing on optimizing your social media profiles. Your profiles serve as the first point of contact for potential customers, so it's crucial to make a strong impression and effectively showcase your brand across various platforms.

To begin, ensure that your profile information is complete and up-to-date. Fill in all the relevant sections, including your bio, website URL, contact information, and location (if applicable). This provides visitors with essential details about your business and makes it easy for them to engage and connect with you.

Craft a compelling and concise bio that encapsulates your brand's essence and value proposition. Use clear and concise language to communicate who you are, what you offer, and why people should follow or engage with your brand. Consider including keywords or hashtags that are relevant to your industry to improve search visibility.

Incorporate visual elements into your profiles to make them visually appealing and instantly recognizable. Use high-quality profile pictures and cover photos that align with your brand's visual identity. Consistency is key, so ensure that your visual elements, such as colors, fonts, and imagery, are consistent across all your social media profiles.

Take advantage of the unique features and customization options offered by each platform. For instance, on Instagram, you can create an Instagram Business Profile and optimize it by adding a call-to-action button, contact information, and relevant industry tags. On LinkedIn, you can showcase your professional expertise by adding your skills, endorsements, and professional achievements.

Utilize keywords and relevant hashtags in your profile descriptions and posts. This helps users discover your brand when they search for specific terms or topics. Conduct keyword research to identify popular and relevant keywords in your industry, and strategically incorporate them into your profiles.

Don't forget to include links to your website or landing pages in your profile descriptions. This encourages visitors to explore your website and take desired actions, such as making a purchase or signing up for a newsletter. Directing traffic from social media to your website is essential for driving conversions and achieving your business goals.

Regularly review and update your profiles to ensure they reflect any changes or updates in your business. This includes updating your contact information, adding new achievements or testimonials, and refreshing your visual elements to maintain a polished and professional appearance.

By optimizing your social media profiles, you create a cohesive and compelling online presence that attracts and engages your target audience. A well-optimized profile increases your credibility, establishes trust, and encourages visitors to explore further and connect with your brand.

Tomorrow, on Day 6, we will explore the process of creating engaging and shareable content. Get ready to captivate your audience with content that resonates and inspires them to take action.

Day 6: Creating Engaging and Shareable Content

Welcome to Day 6 of your 30-day social media growth hack journey for small business owners! Today, we'll be exploring the process of creating engaging and shareable content. Compelling content is the key to capturing the attention of your audience, increasing engagement, and ultimately driving growth for your small business.

To create content that resonates with your audience, it's essential to understand their needs, preferences, and pain points. Refer back to your target audience and buyer personas that you developed on Day 2. Consider the type of content that would be most valuable and relevant to them. This could include educational articles, entertaining videos, inspiring quotes, or practical tips and advice.

Variety is key when it comes to content creation. Experiment with different formats, such as images, videos, infographics, and blog posts, to cater to different preferences and capture the attention of diverse audience segments. Keep in mind that different social media platforms have their own strengths and limitations when it comes to content formats, so adapt your content accordingly.

When crafting your content, focus on providing value to your audience. Whether it's offering insights, solving problems, entertaining, or inspiring, ensure that your content serves a purpose and meets the needs of your audience. This positions your brand as a trusted resource and encourages followers to engage and share your content with others.

Utilize storytelling techniques to make your content more engaging and relatable. Incorporate narratives, personal anecdotes, or real-life examples that connect with your audience on an emotional level. People are more likely to engage with content that evokes emotions and triggers a response.

Consistency is key in maintaining engagement and growing your audience. Create a content calendar and establish a regular posting schedule to ensure a steady flow of content. This helps you stay organized, maintain momentum, and keep your audience coming back for more. Experiment with different posting times and days to identify the optimal times for reaching your target audience.

Encourage interaction and engagement with your content by asking questions, inviting comments, or running contests or giveaways. Respond promptly to comments, messages, and mentions to foster a sense of community and build relationships with your audience.

Don't underestimate the power of visual appeal. Invest in high-quality visuals, such as eye-catching images and well-produced videos, that align with your brand's aesthetic. Use design tools and apps to enhance your visuals and make them stand out in crowded social media feeds.

Lastly, make your content shareable by incorporating social sharing buttons and encouraging your audience to share your content with their networks. Develop content that is valuable, entertaining, or informative enough for people to want to share it with others. This expands your reach, increases brand visibility, and attracts new followers.

Creating engaging and shareable content is a continuous process of experimentation, refinement, and adaptation. Pay attention to the performance metrics of your content, such as likes, shares, comments, and click-through rates, to gain insights into what resonates most with your audience. Adjust your content strategy based on these insights to continuously improve and drive social media growth.

Tomorrow, on Day 7, we will explore the power of hashtags and how to leverage them effectively for increased reach and engagement. Get ready to discover the hashtag secrets that can elevate your social media presence.

Day 7: Leveraging the Power of Hashtags

Welcome to Day 7 of your 30-day social media growth hack journey for small business owners! Today, we'll be diving into the power of hashtags and how to leverage them effectively for increased reach and engagement. Hashtags play a crucial role in organizing and categorizing content on social media platforms, making them a valuable tool to expand your brand's visibility and connect with your target audience.

To begin, conduct hashtag research to identify relevant and popular hashtags in your industry. Look for hashtags that align with your brand, content, and target audience. Tools like Hashtagify, RiteTag, and Sprout Social can help you find trending and popular hashtags related to your niche.

It's essential to strike a balance between using broad and specific hashtags. Broad hashtags with high search volume, such as #marketing or

#smallbusiness, can expose your content to a larger audience. However, they also face higher competition, making it harder for your content to stand out. On the other hand, specific hashtags, like #socialmediatipsforbusiness or #handmadejewelry, may have a smaller audience but offer a more targeted reach.

Consider using a mix of both broad and specific hashtags to optimize your content's discoverability. This allows you to reach a larger audience while still targeting people who are more likely to be interested in your specific niche.

Once you've identified relevant hashtags, incorporate them strategically into your social media posts. Limit the number of hashtags to a reasonable amount, as overcrowding your posts with too many hashtags can appear spammy and reduce the quality of your content. Aim for a balance of 5-10 hashtags per post, depending on the platform and the content.

Ensure that the hashtags you use are relevant to the content and context of your posts.

Irrelevant or misleading hashtags can harm your credibility and make it harder for your target audience to find you. Take the time to research and understand the hashtags you use to ensure they align with your brand and resonate with your target audience.

Track the performance of your hashtag usage to gauge their effectiveness. Pay attention to metrics like reach, impressions, engagement, and follower growth to identify which hashtags are driving the most engagement and generating the desired results. This data will help you refine your hashtag strategy and identify the most effective hashtags for your brand.

In addition to using existing hashtags, consider creating branded hashtags specific to your business. Branded hashtags help you build a community around your brand, encourage user-generated content, and make it easier for followers to find and engage with your content. Use your brand name, slogan, or a unique phrase that represents your brand as a branded hashtag.

Don't limit your hashtag usage to just the caption of your posts. Incorporate hashtags in your stories, bio, and comments as well. This expands the reach of your content and increases its discoverability across different areas of the platform.

Remember, hashtags are not a one-time setup. Continuously monitor and adapt your hashtag strategy based on changing trends, industry conversations, and the preferences of your target audience. Stay up to date with popular hashtags and adjust your content and hashtag usage accordingly.

By leveraging the power of hashtags effectively, you can significantly increase the visibility, reach, and engagement of your social media content. Hashtags connect you with your target audience, expose your brand to new users, and facilitate engagement within your community.

Tomorrow, on Day 8, we will explore the importance of engaging with your audience and building meaningful connections on social media. Get ready to foster relationships and create a loyal community of followers.

Day 8: Engaging with Your Audience and Building Meaningful Connections

Welcome to Day 8 of your 30-day social media growth hack journey for small business owners! Today, we'll be exploring the importance of engaging with your audience and building meaningful connections on social media. Engaging with your audience goes beyond posting content—it involves actively interacting with your followers, fostering relationships, and creating a loyal community.

Responding to comments, messages, and mentions in a timely manner is crucial. When followers take the time to engage with your content or reach out to you, it's important to acknowledge their efforts and provide meaningful responses. Prompt and personalized responses show that you value your audience and are committed to building relationships.

Encourage conversations by asking questions, soliciting opinions, or seeking feedback. This not only sparks engagement but also makes your audience feel involved and valued. Respond to comments with genuine interest and provide thoughtful responses that add value to the conversation. By actively participating in discussions, you show that you are accessible and interested in what your audience has to say.

Monitor your social media accounts for mentions and tags related to your brand. When someone mentions your business or includes you in a post, take the opportunity to engage with them. Like, comment, or share their content to show your appreciation and support. This helps strengthen relationships and encourages others to mention and tag your brand in their posts.

Show gratitude and appreciation for your followers. Take the time to thank them for their support, comments, or feedback. Consider running special promotions or exclusive giveaways for your loyal followers to show your appreciation. Rewarding your audience fosters loyalty and encourages them to stay engaged with your brand.

Embrace user-generated content (UGC) and encourage your audience to create and share content related to your brand. UGC not only increases engagement but also serves as social proof for your business. Repost or share UGC on your own social media accounts, giving credit to the original creator. This not only showcases your audience's creativity but also builds a sense of community and encourages others to contribute.

Collaborate with influencers or industry experts to expand your reach and tap into their existing audience. Influencer marketing allows you to leverage the credibility and reach of influencers to promote your brand and connect with their followers. Find influencers whose values align with your brand and collaborate on content or campaigns that provide value to both your audience and theirs.

Stay active in relevant communities and groups on social media platforms. Join groups or participate in discussions that are related to your industry or target audience. Share your expertise, provide valuable insights, and engage with other members. This helps establish your authority and builds credibility within your niche.

Consistently monitor social media analytics to gain insights into your audience's behavior and preferences. Analyze engagement metrics such as likes, comments, shares, and click-through rates to understand what type of content resonates most with your audience. Use this information to refine your content strategy and tailor your approach to better meet your audience's needs.

Remember, building meaningful connections on social media is an ongoing process. Consistency, authenticity, and genuine interest in your audience are key. By actively engaging with your followers, fostering relationships, and creating a sense of community, you establish a loyal and dedicated following that supports and advocates for your brand.

Tomorrow, on Day 9, we will delve into the world of social media advertising and how it can help you reach a wider audience and drive growth for your business. Get ready to unlock the potential of targeted advertising on social media platforms.

Day 9: Harnessing the Power of Social Media Advertising

Welcome to Day 9 of your 30-day social media growth hack journey for small business owners! Today, we'll be delving into the world of social media advertising and exploring how it can help you reach a wider audience and drive growth for your business. Social media platforms offer powerful advertising tools that allow you to target specific demographics, increase brand visibility, and generate leads.

Social media advertising provides a cost-effective way to reach a highly targeted audience. Platforms like Facebook, Instagram, Twitter, and LinkedIn offer robust advertising platforms with advanced targeting options. Take advantage of these tools to define your audience based on demographics, interests, behaviors, and even location. This ensures that your ads are seen by the people most likely to be interested in your products or services.

Before you begin advertising, clearly define your campaign objectives. Are you looking to increase brand awareness, drive traffic to your website, generate leads, or boost sales? Having clear goals in mind helps you design and optimize your ads to achieve the desired outcomes.

Craft compelling ad content that captures attention and resonates with your target audience. Develop eye-catching visuals, compelling copy, and clear calls to action. Tailor your messaging to address the pain points and needs of your audience, emphasizing how your products or services can solve their problems or enhance their lives.

Experiment with different ad formats to see what works best for your business. Social media platforms offer various ad formats, including image ads, video ads, carousel ads, and sponsored content. Test different formats to

identify which ones generate the most
engagement and conversions for your business.

Track and analyze the performance of your ads
using the analytics tools provided by the social
media platforms. Monitor key metrics such as
impressions, click-through rates, conversions,
and return on ad spend (ROAS). This data helps
you understand the effectiveness of your ads
and make data-driven decisions to optimize
your campaigns.

Utilize retargeting to re-engage users who have
previously interacted with your brand.
Retargeting allows you to display ads to people
who have visited your website, engaged with
your content, or interacted with your social
media profiles. This helps keep your brand top
of mind and encourages users to take the
desired action.

Don't forget to A/B test your ads to refine your
targeting, messaging, and creative elements.
Split testing allows you to compare different
versions of your ads and determine which
variations perform better. Test different

headlines, visuals, call-to-action buttons, or ad placements to continuously improve the effectiveness of your campaigns.

Allocate a budget for social media advertising and monitor your spend carefully. Start with a conservative budget and increase it gradually as you see positive results. Regularly review the performance of your campaigns and adjust your budget allocation to focus on the most successful ads and targeting options.

Social media advertising is a dynamic and ever-evolving field, so it's essential to stay updated on the latest trends, features, and best practices. Keep an eye on industry news, attend webinars or conferences, and follow relevant thought leaders to stay ahead of the curve.

By harnessing the power of social media advertising, you can expand your reach, attract new customers, and drive growth for your small business. It allows you to leverage the targeting capabilities of social media platforms and deliver your message directly to the right audience at the right time.

Tomorrow, on Day 10, we will explore the world of influencer marketing and how collaborating with influencers can amplify your brand's reach and impact. Get ready to tap into the power of influencers to drive social media growth for your small business.

Day 10: Amplifying Your Reach with Influencer Marketing

Welcome to Day 10 of your 30-day social media growth hack journey for small business owners! Today, we'll be exploring the world of influencer marketing and how collaborating with influencers can amplify your brand's reach and impact. Influencer marketing has gained tremendous popularity in recent years as an effective strategy to tap into the loyal and engaged audiences of social media influencers.

Influencers are individuals who have established credibility, expertise, and a significant following in a specific niche. They have built trust and influence among their followers, making them valuable partners for promoting products or services. Collaborating with influencers allows you to leverage their reach, credibility, and influence to increase brand awareness and drive engagement.

The first step in influencer marketing is to identify the right influencers for your brand. Look for influencers who align with your industry, target audience, and brand values. Consider their content quality, engagement rate, follower demographics, and overall authenticity. Tools like BuzzSumo, Traackr, and Upfluence can help you discover and evaluate potential influencers.

When reaching out to influencers, personalize your communication and explain why you believe a partnership would be beneficial for both parties. Highlight how your brand aligns with their content and audience, and propose a mutually beneficial collaboration. This could include sponsored posts, product reviews, giveaways, or content collaborations.

Ensure that the influencer's audience is genuine and engaged. Look for indicators of real engagement, such as likes, comments, shares, and meaningful interactions. Pay attention to the quality of the comments and the level of engagement on their posts. High-quality engagement indicates an active and loyal

audience that is more likely to be receptive to
your brand's message.

Work closely with the influencer to develop
compelling content that resonates with their
audience and aligns with your brand. Provide
clear guidelines and objectives for the
collaboration, but also allow the influencer
creative freedom to maintain their authenticity.
Co-create content that integrates your brand
naturally and provides value to the influencer's
audience.

Track the performance of influencer campaigns
to measure their impact and effectiveness.
Monitor metrics such as reach, engagement,
click-through rates, and conversions to assess
the success of the collaboration. Analyze the
ROI (return on investment) of each influencer
partnership to determine the value it brings to
your business.

In addition to one-off collaborations, consider
establishing long-term relationships with
influencers. Long-term partnerships allow for
deeper integration of your brand into the

influencer's content and foster a sense of authenticity and trust. Building ongoing relationships with influencers can lead to increased brand loyalty, repeated exposure, and continuous engagement with their audience.

Engage with the influencer's content and their audience to strengthen the relationship. Like, comment, and share their posts to show your support and appreciation. Respond to comments on their posts and engage with their followers, providing valuable insights and building connections.

Remember to comply with disclosure guidelines and regulations regarding sponsored content. Ensure that influencer collaborations are transparent and clearly labeled as sponsored or paid partnerships. This maintains trust with the influencer's audience and adheres to ethical practices in influencer marketing.

As influencer marketing continues to evolve, stay informed about emerging trends, new platforms, and best practices. Follow industry blogs, attend conferences, and engage in discussions to stay ahead of the curve and leverage the latest strategies.

By harnessing the power of influencer marketing, you can tap into the engaged and loyal audiences of influencers, amplify your brand's reach, and drive social media growth for your small business.

Tomorrow, on Day 11, we will explore the potential of video content and how it can enhance your social media presence. Get ready to unlock the power of visual storytelling through videos.

Day 11: The Power of Video Content for Social Media

Welcome to Day 11 of your 30-day social media growth hack journey for small business owners! Today, we'll be diving into the world of video content and exploring how it can enhance your social media presence. Video has become a dominant form of content on social media platforms, offering a powerful medium for storytelling, engagement, and brand promotion.

Video content has the ability to captivate and engage audiences like no other format. It allows you to convey your brand's message in a more dynamic and immersive way, capturing attention and generating higher levels of engagement. Incorporating video into your social media strategy can help you stand out from the competition and leave a lasting impression on your audience.

One of the most popular forms of video content on social media is short-form videos. Platforms like TikTok, Instagram Reels, and Snapchat offer opportunities to create and share engaging videos in a bite-sized format. These videos often feature quick, entertaining, and informative content that is easily consumable and shareable. Experiment with these platforms to create engaging and viral videos that resonate with your target audience.

Live streaming has also gained significant popularity on social media platforms. Live videos allow you to connect with your audience in real-time, fostering a sense of authenticity and immediacy. Use live streaming to host Q&A sessions, product demonstrations, behind-the-scenes glimpses, or live events. Encourage your audience to interact, ask questions, and participate in the live stream, creating an interactive and engaging experience.

Educational and tutorial videos are highly valuable for your audience. Create videos that provide valuable information, tips, and tutorials related to your industry or niche. Position yourself as an expert and a trusted resource by sharing your knowledge and expertise through video content. These videos not only showcase your expertise but also establish your brand as a reliable source of information.

Storytelling is a powerful tool in video content creation. Use videos to tell compelling stories about your brand, products, or customers. Craft narratives that resonate with your audience's emotions, values, and aspirations. By connecting on an emotional level, you can build a deeper connection with your audience and leave a lasting impact.

Incorporate user-generated video content into your social media strategy. Encourage your audience to create and share videos featuring your products or services. This not only increases engagement but also serves as social proof and builds a sense of community around your brand. Repost or share user-generated videos, giving credit to the creators, to showcase the positive experiences of your customers.

Optimize your videos for each social media platform to maximize their impact. Different platforms have varying specifications and requirements for video content. Ensure that your videos are optimized for each platform's aspect ratio, video length, and recommended file formats. This ensures that your videos appear as intended and are fully optimized for the best viewing experience.

Monitor the performance of your video content using social media analytics. Pay attention to metrics such as views, watch time, engagement, and shares. Analyze the data to understand which types of videos perform best with your audience and refine your video content strategy accordingly. Experiment with different video formats, themes, and styles to identify the most effective content for your brand.

Stay up to date with video trends and emerging features on social media platforms. Platforms like Instagram, Facebook, and YouTube are constantly introducing new features and tools to enhance video content creation and sharing. Embrace these new features and experiment with different formats to keep your content fresh, innovative, and aligned with current trends.

By harnessing the power of video content, you can create engaging, memorable, and shareable experiences for your audience. Videos have the potential to reach a wider audience, increase brand awareness, and drive social media growth for your small business.

Tomorrow, on Day 12, we will explore the world of social media contests and how they can boost engagement and attract new followers. Get ready to unlock the potential of interactive and exciting contests on social media platforms.

Day 12: Boosting Engagement with Social Media Contests

Welcome to Day 12 of your 30-day social media growth hack journey for small business owners! Today, we'll be exploring the world of social media contests and how they can boost engagement, attract new followers, and create buzz around your brand. Social media contests are a powerful strategy to encourage participation, reward your audience, and generate excitement.

Contests create a sense of excitement and anticipation among your audience. They provide an incentive for people to engage with your brand and participate in a fun and interactive experience. Contests can take various forms, such as photo contests, caption contests, sweepstakes, giveaways, or challenges. Choose a contest format that aligns with your brand, resonates with your target audience, and encourages user-generated content.

Define clear goals for your contest. Are you aiming to increase brand awareness, generate user-generated content, attract new followers, or drive website traffic? Having clear objectives helps you design and execute a contest that aligns with your overall marketing goals and measures its success.

Choose enticing prizes that are relevant to your audience and align with your brand. The prize should be valuable enough to attract participation and motivate your audience to take action. Consider partnering with other businesses or influencers to provide joint prizes, which can expand your reach and tap into their audiences as well.

Create clear and concise contest rules. Clearly outline the entry requirements, eligibility criteria, and the duration of the contest. Specify how winners will be selected and announced, and provide a timeline for prize fulfillment. Transparent and well-communicated rules build trust and ensure a fair contest.

Promote your contest across your social media channels and other marketing channels. Use visually appealing graphics, videos, and catchy captions to grab attention and generate excitement. Leverage the power of social media advertising to reach a wider audience beyond your existing followers. Encourage your audience to share the contest with their friends and networks, increasing its visibility and potential reach.

Encourage user-generated content as part of your contest. Ask participants to create and share content related to your brand, products, or services. This not only generates valuable content for your brand but also increases engagement and strengthens brand loyalty. User-generated content can also serve as social proof, showcasing positive experiences and testimonials from your customers.

Engage with participants throughout the contest. Respond to comments, answer questions, and provide updates and reminders. Show appreciation for participants' efforts and acknowledge their contributions. This level of engagement builds a positive relationship with your audience and encourages ongoing participation.

Consider incorporating voting mechanisms into your contest. Allowing participants or the general public to vote for their favorite entries creates a sense of competition and involvement. This can also generate additional engagement and excitement as participants rally their friends and followers to vote for them.

Announce the winners promptly and publicly. Congratulate the winners and thank all participants for their engagement. Consider sharing the winning entries on your social media platforms, giving credit to the creators. This not only recognizes the winners but also showcases the creativity and talent within your community.

Follow up after the contest to maintain engagement and momentum. Share behind-the-scenes content, interviews with winners, or testimonials from participants. Consider offering exclusive discounts or promotions to participants as a token of appreciation. This keeps the excitement alive and encourages continued engagement with your brand.

Monitor the performance of your contest using social media analytics. Track metrics such as engagement levels, reach, follower growth, and website traffic during the contest period. Analyze the data to gain insights into the effectiveness of your contest and make informed decisions for future campaigns.

Social media contests provide an excellent opportunity to boost engagement, attract new followers, and create a positive buzz around your brand. By designing compelling contests, providing enticing prizes, and engaging with your audience throughout the process, you can create an exciting and rewarding experience for your community.

Tomorrow, on Day 13, we will delve into the world of social media advertising and explore how paid ads can help you reach a targeted audience and accelerate your social media growth. Get ready to unlock the power of targeted advertising on social media platforms.

Day 13: Accelerating Growth with Social Media Advertising

Welcome to Day 13 of your 30-day social media growth hack journey for small business owners! Today, we'll be delving into the world of social media advertising and exploring how paid ads can help you reach a targeted audience and accelerate your social media growth. Social media advertising offers powerful tools and targeting options to effectively promote your brand, products, or services to a specific audience.

Social media platforms like Facebook, Instagram, Twitter, LinkedIn, and Pinterest provide robust advertising platforms with sophisticated targeting capabilities. By investing in social media ads, you can reach a wider audience, increase brand visibility, drive website traffic, and ultimately, boost your business's growth.

To begin, define your advertising goals. Are you looking to increase brand awareness, drive traffic to your website, generate leads, or boost sales? Clarifying your objectives will guide your advertising strategy and help you measure the success of your campaigns.

Understand your target audience and create detailed buyer personas. Consider demographics, interests, behaviors, and psychographics of your ideal customers. Social media platforms offer powerful targeting options to ensure your ads are seen by the right people. Refine your audience based on factors like age, gender, location, interests, job titles, and more, depending on the platform you choose.

Select the most suitable social media platform for your advertising campaign. Each platform has its unique user base and features. For example, Facebook and Instagram offer highly visual ad formats, Twitter allows for real-time conversations, and LinkedIn targets professionals and B2B audiences. Choose the platform(s) that align with your audience demographics and campaign objectives.

Design compelling ad creatives that capture attention and drive engagement. Use eye-catching visuals, clear and concise copy, and compelling call-to-action (CTA) buttons. Experiment with different ad formats such as image ads, video ads, carousel ads, or interactive ads, depending on the platform's capabilities. A/B test different variations of your ads to identify the most effective combinations.

Leverage the targeting options provided by social media platforms. Take advantage of advanced targeting features like custom audiences, lookalike audiences, and retargeting. Custom audiences allow you to target specific groups based on their engagement with your brand, such as website visitors or email subscribers. Lookalike audiences help you reach new users who have similar characteristics to your existing customers. Retargeting allows you to re-engage with users who have previously interacted with your brand but haven't converted.

Set a budget for your advertising campaigns. Start with a conservative budget and monitor the performance of your ads. As you gather data and optimize your campaigns, you can gradually increase your budget to scale your advertising efforts. Monitor key metrics like click-through rates (CTR), cost per click (CPC), conversion rates, and return on ad spend (ROAS) to evaluate the effectiveness of your campaigns.

Continuously monitor and optimize your ads. Regularly review the performance of your campaigns and make data-driven decisions. Adjust your targeting, ad creatives, or bidding strategies based on the insights you gather. Experiment with different ad placements, ad schedules, and audience segments to find the winning combination for your brand.

Track and measure the results of your advertising campaigns using social media analytics and conversion tracking tools. Monitor metrics such as impressions, clicks, conversions, cost per conversion, and ROI to assess the success of your ads. Analyze the data to understand what resonates with your audience and refine your advertising strategy accordingly.

Stay up to date with the latest trends and features in social media advertising. Social media platforms constantly introduce new ad formats, targeting options, and optimization tools. Keep an eye on industry updates, attend webinars or training sessions, and experiment with new features to stay ahead of the curve and maximize your advertising results.

Social media advertising offers a powerful way to accelerate your social media growth and reach your target audience effectively. By strategically investing in paid ads, targeting the right audience, and continuously optimizing your campaigns, you can drive brand awareness, attract new customers, and boost your business's growth.

Tomorrow, on Day 14, we will explore the world of influencer marketing and how collaborating with influencers can expand your reach and increase your brand's credibility. Get ready to tap into the power of influencer partnerships on social media.

Day 14: Expanding Reach with Influencer Marketing

Welcome to Day 14 of your 30-day social media growth hack journey for small business owners! Today, we'll be exploring the world of influencer marketing and how collaborating with influencers can help you expand your reach, increase brand awareness, and enhance your brand's credibility on social media.

Influencer marketing has become a popular and effective strategy for brands to leverage the influence and reach of social media personalities to promote their products or services. Influencers are individuals who have built a dedicated following on social media platforms and have the power to sway their audience's opinions and purchasing decisions.

Here's how you can harness the power of influencer marketing to accelerate your social media growth:

Identify relevant influencers: Start by identifying influencers in your industry or niche who align with your brand values and target audience. Look for influencers with a sizable and engaged following. Consider factors such as their content quality, engagement rates, and authenticity.

Build relationships: Engage with influencers by following them, liking their content, and leaving thoughtful comments. Establish a genuine connection and build a relationship before reaching out for collaboration. Engaging with their content also increases your chances of getting noticed by the influencer.

Define campaign objectives: Clearly define your objectives for the influencer collaboration. Are you aiming to increase brand awareness, drive traffic to your website, boost sales, or reach a new audience? Having a clear objective will help you choose the right influencers and measure the success of your campaign.

Collaborate creatively: Work with influencers to create compelling content that showcases your brand in an authentic and engaging way. Discuss ideas and come up with creative ways to promote your products or services. Give influencers creative freedom while aligning the content with your brand's messaging and goals.

Track performance: Monitor the performance of your influencer campaigns using trackable links, unique discount codes, or dedicated landing pages. This allows you to measure the impact of the collaboration in terms of reach, engagement, website traffic, and conversions. Analyze the data to refine your influencer marketing strategy.

Micro-influencers: Consider working with micro-influencers who have a smaller following but a highly engaged and loyal audience. Micro-influencers often have a niche focus and can provide a more targeted reach. Collaborating with micro-influencers can be cost-effective and yield impressive results.

Long-term partnerships: Building long-term relationships with influencers can be beneficial for both parties. Instead of one-off collaborations, consider ongoing partnerships where influencers become ambassadors for your brand. This helps create a consistent and recognizable brand presence among their audience.

Transparency and authenticity: Transparency is key in influencer marketing. Ensure that influencer collaborations are disclosed clearly to maintain transparency with your audience. Authenticity is also crucial, so work with influencers who genuinely appreciate your brand and can provide an authentic endorsement.

Engage with the influencer's audience: When an influencer promotes your brand, actively engage with their audience through comments, likes, and replies. Respond to any questions or inquiries promptly and provide a positive experience. Engaging with the influencer's audience builds trust and encourages further interaction with your brand.

User-generated content: Encourage influencers and their audience to create user-generated content featuring your products or services. This not only extends the reach of your brand but also fosters a sense of community and trust around your products. Repost or share user-generated content, giving credit to the creators, to showcase the positive experiences of your customers.

Influencer marketing can be a powerful tool to expand your brand's reach, increase engagement, and build credibility on social media. By collaborating with influencers who resonate with your target audience, creating compelling content, and fostering authentic relationships, you can accelerate your social media growth and drive meaningful results for your small business.

Tomorrow, on Day 15, we will explore the concept of social media collaborations and how partnering with other businesses or content creators can mutually benefit your growth efforts. Get ready to unlock the potential of collaboration on social media!

Day 15: Harnessing the Power of Social Media Collaborations

Welcome to Day 15 of your 30-day social media growth hack journey for small business owners! Today, we'll be diving into the concept of social media collaborations and exploring how partnering with other businesses or content creators can mutually benefit your growth efforts. Social media collaborations offer a unique opportunity to tap into new audiences, increase brand visibility, and create valuable content.

Collaborating with other businesses or content creators on social media can take various forms, including joint campaigns, guest posts, co-created content, or cross-promotions. Here's how you can harness the power of social media collaborations to accelerate your growth:

Identify complementary brands: Look for businesses or content creators in your industry or niche that offer complementary products, services, or content. Choose partners whose audience aligns with your target market. Collaborating with complementary brands allows you to tap into a relevant and engaged audience that may be interested in your offerings.

Set clear goals: Define your goals for the collaboration. Are you aiming to expand your reach, increase brand awareness, drive traffic to your website, or boost sales? Having clear objectives will guide your collaboration strategy and help measure its success.

Establish mutual benefits: Ensure that the collaboration offers mutual benefits for both parties involved. Identify what each partner brings to the table and how they can support each other's growth. This could include sharing resources, leveraging each other's networks, or co-creating valuable content.

Plan the collaboration: Collaborate with your partners to plan the details of the collaboration. Determine the scope, timeline, and specific activities involved. Consider creating a content calendar or a joint campaign plan to ensure a cohesive and coordinated effort.

Co-create content: One powerful way to collaborate is by co-creating content. This could involve guest blog posts, joint videos, podcasts, or social media takeovers. By combining your expertise and resources, you can create compelling and valuable content that resonates with both audiences.

Cross-promote: Promote each other's brands or content through your respective social media channels. This can include sharing posts, tagging each other, or featuring each other in your stories. Cross-promotion exposes your brand to a new audience and encourages your existing audience to explore your partner's offerings.

Run joint campaigns: Consider running joint campaigns or giveaways where participants have the opportunity to win prizes or discounts from both brands. This encourages audience engagement, expands your reach, and increases brand visibility.

Leverage influencer collaborations: Collaborating with influencers who align with both brands can amplify the impact of your collaboration. Influencers can help generate buzz, reach new audiences, and provide authentic endorsements for your collaborative efforts.

Measure and evaluate: Track the performance of your collaboration using social media analytics. Monitor metrics such as engagement, reach, website traffic, and conversions to assess the success of your collaboration. Evaluate what worked well and what could be improved for future collaborations.

Nurture long-term partnerships: Building long-term partnerships with other businesses or content creators can create a network of support and continuous growth. Explore opportunities for ongoing collaborations, such as co-hosting events, sharing resources, or launching joint products or services.

Social media collaborations offer a powerful
way to expand your reach, tap into new
audiences, and create valuable content. By
identifying complementary brands, setting clear
goals, planning collaboratively, and promoting
each other's offerings, you can amplify your
social media growth and achieve mutually
beneficial results.

Tomorrow, on Day 16, we will explore the world
of user-generated content and how it can fuel
your social media growth. Get ready to unlock
the potential of your community's creativity!

Day 16: Fueling Growth with User-Generated Content

Welcome to Day 16 of your 30-day social media growth hack journey for small business owners! Today, we'll be delving into the world of user-generated content (UGC) and how it can be a powerful tool to fuel your social media growth. User-generated content refers to any form of content created by your audience or customers that showcases their experiences with your brand.

UGC is highly valuable for businesses because it provides authentic and genuine content that resonates with your target audience. It fosters a sense of community, trust, and loyalty around your brand. Here's how you can harness the power of user-generated content to accelerate your social media growth:

Encourage and incentivize UGC: Motivate your audience to create and share content related to your brand. You can do this by running contests, giveaways, or challenges that

encourage users to submit content for a chance
to win prizes or get featured on your social
media channels. Offer incentives that align with
your brand and appeal to your audience's
interests.

Create a branded hashtag: Establish a unique
and catchy branded hashtag that represents
your brand or a specific campaign. Encourage
your audience to use this hashtag when posting
content related to your products or services. A
branded hashtag not only helps you track UGC
but also creates a sense of community around
your brand.

Showcase UGC on your channels: Regularly
feature user-generated content on your social
media channels. Repost photos, videos, or
testimonials from satisfied customers. This not
only provides social proof but also encourages
others to share their experiences with your
brand.

Engage with UGC creators: Show appreciation
to those who create UGC by acknowledging and
engaging with their content. Like their posts,

leave comments, and thank them for their
support. Building a relationship with UGC
creators fosters a positive brand perception and
encourages others to participate.

Run UGC-driven campaigns: Design campaigns
centered around user-generated content. For
example, you could ask your audience to submit
creative product usage ideas or share their
favorite moments with your brand. Showcase
the best submissions and reward participants.
UGC-driven campaigns generate excitement
and participation while generating valuable
content.

Highlight customer stories: Share compelling
customer stories or testimonials that highlight
the impact of your products or services on their
lives. Authentic and emotional storytelling can
significantly influence your audience and drive
engagement.

Leverage Stories and Reels: Utilize the "Stories"
feature on platforms like Instagram and
Facebook to curate UGC collections or
behind-the-scenes content. Additionally, with

the popularity of short-form video content,
consider using Instagram Reels to showcase
UGC in a fun and creative way.

Listen to your audience: Actively listen to what
your audience is saying about your brand on
social media. Respond to comments, messages,
and mentions promptly. Acknowledge
feedback, both positive and constructive, and
use it to improve your products or services.

Provide guidelines for UGC: While encouraging
UGC creativity, provide guidelines to ensure
that the content aligns with your brand values
and standards. Clearly state what kind of
content you're looking for and any specific rules
for participation.

Repurpose UGC in marketing efforts: Don't
limit the use of UGC to social media alone.
Repurpose high-quality UGC in your email
marketing, website, and other marketing
materials to provide social proof and reinforce
your brand's credibility.

User-generated content is a powerful tool for social media growth as it engages your audience, builds trust, and showcases authentic experiences with your brand. By encouraging UGC, showcasing it on your channels, and using it creatively in your marketing efforts, you can harness its potential to fuel your social media growth.

Tomorrow, on Day 17, we will explore the importance of social listening and how it can help you understand your audience better and refine your social media strategy. Get ready to tune in and listen to what your audience is saying!

Day 17: Harnessing the Power of Social Listening

Welcome to Day 17 of your 30-day social media growth hack journey for small business owners! Today, we'll be exploring the importance of social listening and how it can help you understand your audience better, refine your social media strategy, and drive meaningful growth.

Social listening refers to the process of monitoring and analyzing conversations and mentions about your brand, industry, or relevant topics on social media platforms. It involves actively listening to what your audience is saying, understanding their needs and preferences, and using that information to inform your social media strategy. Here's how you can harness the power of social listening to accelerate your growth:

Monitor brand mentions: Keep a close eye on social media platforms to track mentions of your brand. This includes direct mentions of your brand's handle, as well as mentions without tagging. Use social listening tools or set up alerts to receive notifications whenever your brand is mentioned. Respond to mentions promptly, whether they are positive or negative, to show that you value your audience's feedback.

Understand audience sentiment: Social listening allows you to gauge the sentiment surrounding your brand. Analyze the tone and emotions expressed in mentions and comments to understand how your audience feels about your products, services, or marketing campaigns. This insight can help you identify areas of improvement and address any concerns or issues.

Identify trends and industry insights: By monitoring conversations related to your industry or niche, you can stay updated on the latest trends, news, and topics of interest. This helps you position your brand as a thought leader and allows you to create relevant and timely content that resonates with your audience.

Engage in conversations: Actively engage in conversations related to your brand or industry. Respond to comments, answer questions, and participate in discussions. This not only strengthens your relationship with your audience but also provides an opportunity to showcase your expertise and add value to the conversation.

Identify influencers and brand advocates: Through social listening, you can identify individuals who frequently mention your brand in a positive light or act as brand advocates. Engage with these influencers and advocates, nurture relationships with them, and explore potential collaborations or partnerships. Their endorsement can significantly boost your brand's visibility and credibility.

Discover customer pain points and preferences: Social listening allows you to uncover your audience's pain points, challenges, and preferences. Pay attention to recurring themes or concerns expressed in comments and messages. Use this valuable insight to address customer needs, refine your products or services, and develop targeted marketing campaigns.

Refine your content strategy: Analyzing the type of content that resonates with your audience can help you refine your content strategy. Identify the topics, formats, and styles that generate high engagement and interest. Use this knowledge to create more of the content your audience craves, driving higher levels of engagement and growth.

Track competitors: Social listening isn't just about monitoring your own brand; it also involves keeping an eye on your competitors. Track their social media presence, monitor their campaigns, and analyze audience sentiment towards their brand. This helps you identify gaps in the market, spot opportunities, and differentiate your brand from competitors.

Use social listening tools: Utilize social listening tools and analytics platforms to streamline the process. These tools can help you monitor conversations, track brand mentions, and analyze sentiment at scale. They provide valuable insights and save time by automating certain aspects of social listening.

Adapt and optimize your strategy: Based on the insights gained from social listening, adapt and optimize your social media strategy. Make data-driven decisions regarding content creation, audience targeting, and campaign optimization. Continuously refine your approach to better serve your audience's needs and preferences.

Social listening is a valuable practice that empowers you to understand your audience, uncover insights, and refine your social media strategy. By actively listening to what your audience is saying, engaging in conversations, and leveraging social listening tools, you can drive meaningful growth for your small business.

Tomorrow, on Day 18, we will explore the power of visual content and how you can leverage it to capture your audience's attention and drive engagement on social media. Get ready to unleash your creativity!

Day 18: Unleashing the Power of Visual Content

Welcome to Day 18 of your 30-day social media growth hack journey for small business owners! Today, we'll be exploring the power of visual content and how you can leverage it to capture your audience's attention, drive engagement, and propel your social media growth.

Visual content is a powerful tool in your social media arsenal. It has the ability to convey messages, evoke emotions, and tell compelling stories in a captivating and memorable way. Here are some strategies to help you unleash the power of visual content:

Use high-quality imagery: Invest in high-quality images that are visually appealing and reflect your brand's identity. Whether it's product photos, lifestyle images, or behind-the-scenes shots, make sure they are well-lit, clear, and professional. High-quality imagery not only grabs attention but also enhances your brand's credibility.

Leverage videos: Videos are an engaging and popular form of visual content on social media. Create short videos that showcase your products, provide tutorials, share customer testimonials, or tell stories related to your brand. Experiment with different formats, such as product demos, interviews, or animated videos, to keep your content fresh and diverse.

Tell visual stories: Use visual content to tell stories that resonate with your audience. Storytelling through images or videos creates an emotional connection and helps your audience relate to your brand. Consider using a series of visuals to convey a narrative or share user-generated content that showcases real-life experiences with your brand.

Infographics and data visualization: Infographics are an effective way to present complex information or data in a visually appealing and easy-to-understand format. Create infographics that highlight industry statistics, provide tips, or offer valuable insights. This not only captures attention but also positions your brand as an authoritative source of information.

Create shareable and relatable content: Visual content that is relatable and shareable has the potential to go viral and reach a wider audience. Create content that elicits emotions, makes people laugh, or taps into current trends or popular culture. Encourage your audience to share and tag their friends, increasing the visibility of your brand.

Embrace visual branding: Develop a consistent visual branding strategy that reflects your brand's personality and values. Use consistent colors, fonts, and design elements across your visual content to create a cohesive and recognizable brand identity. This helps build brand recognition and reinforces your brand's message and values.

Optimize for each platform: Different social media platforms have unique requirements and formats for visual content. Optimize your visuals to fit each platform's specifications, whether it's adjusting the dimensions for images or creating vertical videos for platforms like Instagram Stories or TikTok. Tailoring your visual content to each platform ensures optimal visibility and engagement.

Incorporate user-generated content: User-generated content is a powerful form of visual content that can drive engagement and build trust. Encourage your audience to share their photos or videos featuring your products or brand. Repost and showcase this content, giving credit to the creators. User-generated content not only diversifies your visual content but also fosters a sense of community around your brand.

Experiment with different formats: Don't be afraid to try different formats and styles of visual content. Test out carousel posts, GIFs, cinemagraphs, or interactive images to add variety to your content mix. Experimentation keeps your audience engaged and allows you to discover what resonates best with them.

Analyze and iterate: Regularly analyze the performance of your visual content using social media analytics. Monitor metrics such as reach, engagement, and click-through rates to understand what visuals are resonating with your audience. Use these insights to refine your visual content strategy and optimize for better results.

Visual content has the power to capture attention, evoke emotions, and drive engagement on social media. By leveraging high-quality imagery, videos, storytelling, and user-generated content, you can create a visually compelling brand presence that fuels your social media growth.

Tomorrow, on Day 19, we will explore the importance of collaboration and partnerships in growing your social media presence. Get ready to connect with others and expand your reach!

Day 19: Expanding Your Reach through Collaboration and Partnerships

Welcome to Day 19 of your 30-day social media growth hack journey for small business owners! Today, we'll be exploring the importance of collaboration and partnerships in expanding your social media reach and growing your presence online.

Collaborating with others in your industry or partnering with influencers and like-minded brands can be a game-changer for your social media growth. By combining audiences and resources, you can tap into new markets, increase your brand exposure, and build valuable relationships. Here are some strategies to help you leverage collaboration and partnerships:

Identify potential collaborators: Look for individuals or brands in your niche or related industries that share similar values and target audiences. Consider businesses with complementary products or services, as well as influencers who have a significant following in your industry. Reach out to them with a well-thought-out collaboration proposal.

Define mutual goals: Before starting a collaboration, clearly define the goals and objectives you want to achieve together. Whether it's increasing brand awareness, driving traffic to your websites, or growing your social media following, aligning on common goals ensures that both parties benefit from the partnership.

Co-create content: Work together to co-create content that resonates with both audiences. This could include joint blog posts, social media campaigns, webinars, or even product collaborations. By combining your expertise and creativity, you can deliver valuable content that engages both your audiences.

Host giveaways and contests: Partner with other brands or influencers to host joint giveaways or contests. This not only encourages audience participation but also exposes your brand to a wider audience. Make sure the prizes align with your target audience's interests to attract the right participants.

Guest posting and takeovers: Collaborate with influencers or industry experts to do guest posts on each other's blogs or social media channels. This allows you to tap into their audience and vice versa, increasing your reach and credibility. Takeovers, where an influencer temporarily takes control of your social media account, can also generate excitement and engagement.

Cross-promote content: Share each other's content on your respective social media channels to introduce your audiences to one another. Cross-promotion extends your brand's reach and exposes you to a new pool of potential followers or customers. Use the opportunity to introduce your partner's brand or influencer's personality to your audience.

Collaborate on events or webinars: Organize joint webinars, live sessions, or virtual events where you can share valuable insights or host discussions relevant to your industry. Co-hosting events fosters a sense of community and positions your brand as a trusted authority in your field.

Measure and analyze results: After the collaboration, analyze the impact of the partnership on your social media growth. Track metrics such as follower growth, engagement, website traffic, and sales to assess the success of the collaboration. Use this data to refine your approach for future partnerships.

Build long-term relationships: Collaboration is not just a one-time affair; it's about building long-term relationships. Nurture the connections you've made and explore opportunities for continued cooperation. Long-term partnerships can lead to recurring benefits and sustained growth.

Be authentic and genuine: When collaborating with others, be authentic and genuine in your interactions. Your audience can spot inauthentic partnerships from afar, which may harm your brand reputation. Choose collaborations that align with your values and add value to your audience's experience.

Collaboration and partnerships can be instrumental in expanding your social media reach and accelerating your growth. By identifying the right partners, defining mutual goals, co-creating valuable content, and fostering long-term relationships, you can tap into new audiences and take your social media presence to new heights.

Tomorrow, on Day 20, we will dive into the world of influencer marketing and how you can leverage it to amplify your brand's reach and engagement. Get ready to connect with influential voices in your industry!

Day 20: Amplifying Your Brand with Influencer Marketing

Welcome to Day 20 of your 30-day social media growth hack journey for small business owners! Today, we'll be exploring the world of influencer marketing and how you can leverage it to amplify your brand's reach, engagement, and overall social media growth.

Influencer marketing has become a powerful strategy for businesses of all sizes to connect with their target audience and gain credibility in the market. By partnering with influencers who have a loyal following and influence over your target demographic, you can tap into their audience, build trust, and drive meaningful results. Here's how you can leverage influencer marketing to amplify your brand:

Identify relevant influencers: Start by identifying influencers in your industry or niche who align with your brand's values and target audience. Look for influencers who have an engaged following and a genuine connection with their audience. Use social listening tools or influencer marketing platforms to discover potential influencers.

Establish your goals: Before reaching out to influencers, define your goals for the influencer marketing campaign. It could be increasing brand awareness, driving website traffic, generating leads, or boosting sales. Clear goals help you determine the type of influencers you need and the metrics you'll use to measure success.

Authentic partnerships: When approaching influencers, focus on building authentic partnerships. Personalize your outreach and demonstrate a genuine interest in their content and audience. Show how your brand's values align with theirs and how the collaboration can benefit both parties and their respective audiences.

Co-create compelling content: Collaborate with influencers to co-create content that resonates with their audience and highlights your brand. Give influencers creative freedom while providing guidelines to ensure alignment with your brand's messaging. Whether it's sponsored posts, reviews, tutorials, or testimonials, aim for authentic and engaging content.

Leverage their expertise: Influencers have a deep understanding of their audience's preferences and interests. Tap into their expertise by seeking their input on content ideas, product development, or campaign strategies. Their insights can provide valuable guidance in tailoring your messaging and offerings to better resonate with your target audience.

Giveaways and promotions: Partner with influencers to host giveaways or run promotions. This encourages their followers to engage with your brand and increases your reach. Create enticing offers or exclusive discounts for the influencer's audience, incentivizing them to take action and drive conversions.

Sponsored content and reviews: Sponsored posts or reviews by influencers can significantly impact your brand's visibility and credibility. Ensure that the sponsored content is clearly disclosed as such to maintain transparency. Encourage influencers to provide honest and genuine feedback about your products or services.

Track and measure performance: Monitor the performance of influencer marketing campaigns using relevant metrics such as reach, engagement, click-through rates, and conversions. Use tracking links or unique discount codes to attribute sales or website traffic generated by specific influencers. Analyze the data to assess the effectiveness of each campaign and make informed decisions for future collaborations.

Micro-influencers and nano-influencers: Don't overlook the power of micro-influencers and nano-influencers. These individuals have smaller but highly engaged and niche-specific audiences. Partnering with micro-influencers allows you to connect with a highly targeted audience, often at a lower cost compared to larger influencers.

Nurture long-term relationships: Building long-term relationships with influencers can be beneficial for sustained growth. Maintain open communication, support their content, and consider ongoing collaborations or ambassador programs. Investing in long-term partnerships allows influencers to become advocates for your brand, building trust and loyalty among their followers.

Influencer marketing can be a valuable tool to amplify your brand's reach, credibility, and social media growth. By partnering with influencers who align with your brand, co-creating compelling content, and tracking the performance of your campaigns, you can tap into their influence and leverage it to achieve your marketing objectives.

Tomorrow, on Day 21, we will explore the power of user-generated content (UGC) and how you can harness it to foster authenticity, engagement, and community on social media. Get ready to empower your audience to become content creators!

Day 21: Harnessing the Power of User-Generated Content (UGC)

Welcome to Day 21 of your 30-day social media growth hack journey for small business owners! Today, we'll be exploring the power of user-generated content (UGC) and how you can harness it to foster authenticity, engagement, and community on social media.

User-generated content refers to any form of content, such as photos, videos, testimonials, or reviews, that is created and shared by your customers or audience. UGC is a powerful tool for small businesses as it not only showcases real-life experiences with your brand but also encourages engagement and builds trust. Here's how you can harness the power of UGC:

Encourage and incentivize UGC: Actively encourage your audience to create and share content related to your brand. This could be through contests, challenges, or simply by asking them to share their experiences using a branded hashtag. Consider offering incentives such as discounts, exclusive access, or the chance to be featured on your social media channels.

Showcase customer testimonials and reviews: Share positive customer testimonials and reviews on your social media platforms. Highlight the experiences and feedback of satisfied customers to build credibility and trust with your audience. This not only encourages engagement but also serves as social proof, influencing others to engage with your brand.

Repost and give credit: When customers or followers create UGC related to your brand, repost their content and give credit. This not only acknowledges their efforts but also strengthens the relationship with your audience. Tag and mention the original creator in your posts to show appreciation and foster a sense of community.

Create UGC campaigns: Develop campaigns specifically designed to generate UGC. This could be asking customers to share their creative uses of your product, their favorite moments with your brand, or stories about how your services have positively impacted their lives. Frame your campaign around a clear call-to-action and make it easy for participants to share their content.

Leverage social media features: Take advantage of social media features that facilitate UGC, such as Instagram's "Ask Me Anything" questions, polls, or story stickers. These interactive features encourage your audience to share their opinions, experiences, or ideas, which can be valuable UGC for your brand.

Engage with UGC creators: When your audience creates UGC, make an effort to engage with them. Like, comment, and respond to their posts to show that you value their contributions. This not only strengthens your relationship with the content creators but also encourages others to participate in creating UGC.

Feature UGC on your website or blog: Showcase UGC on your website or blog to further amplify the voices of your customers. This could be in the form of a dedicated UGC gallery, customer spotlights, or case studies. By featuring UGC on your owned channels, you demonstrate the authenticity and impact of your brand.

Incorporate UGC into your marketing materials: Integrate UGC into your marketing materials, such as email campaigns, product catalogs, or print advertisements. This not only adds a personal touch but also showcases real experiences and testimonials that resonate with potential customers.

Listen to UGC for insights: Pay attention to the UGC your audience creates. It can provide valuable insights into their preferences, challenges, and needs. Use these insights to inform your product development, content strategy, or marketing initiatives, ensuring that you are meeting the expectations of your audience.

Build a UGC community: Foster a community around UGC by creating a dedicated space for your audience to connect and share their experiences. This could be a branded hashtag on social media or a private Facebook group. Encourage conversations, provide support, and celebrate the contributions of your UGC creators.

Harnessing the power of user-generated content can bring authenticity, engagement, and community to your social media channels. By encouraging UGC, showcasing it, and leveraging it in your marketing efforts, you empower your audience to become content creators and advocates for your brand.

Tomorrow, on Day 22, we will dive into the world of social media advertising and how you can effectively use paid ads to fuel your social media growth. Get ready to amplify your reach and drive targeted traffic to your brand!

Day 22: Amplifying Your Reach with Social Media Advertising

Welcome to Day 22 of your 30-day social media growth hack journey for small business owners! Today, we'll be delving into the world of social media advertising and how you can leverage paid ads to amplify your reach, drive targeted traffic, and boost your social media growth.

Social media advertising offers a powerful way to expand your brand's visibility and connect with your target audience on popular platforms like Facebook, Instagram, Twitter, LinkedIn, and more. With the right strategies, you can maximize the impact of your ad campaigns and achieve your marketing objectives. Here's how you can effectively use social media advertising:

Define your objectives: Before diving into social media advertising, clearly define your objectives. Are you looking to increase brand awareness, drive website traffic, generate leads, or boost sales? Understanding your goals will guide your ad campaign strategy and ensure you allocate your budget effectively.

Know your target audience: Identify and understand your target audience's demographics, interests, behaviors, and pain points. This knowledge helps you create highly targeted ad campaigns that resonate with the right people and minimize ad spend wastage.

Choose the right platform: Different social media platforms cater to different audiences and offer various ad formats. Choose the platforms that align with your target audience and campaign objectives. For example, Instagram is ideal for visually appealing ads, while LinkedIn is more suitable for B2B targeting.

Optimize your ad creative: Your ad creative should be visually compelling, on-brand, and attention-grabbing. Use high-quality images or videos, compelling ad copy, and a clear call-to-action. A/B test different creatives to identify which ones resonate best with your audience.

Set a budget and schedule: Determine your advertising budget and schedule your ads strategically. Consider peak times when your target audience is most active on the platform. Start with a smaller budget and scale up once you identify what works best for your campaign.

Utilize targeting options: Take advantage of the various targeting options provided by social media platforms. You can target based on demographics, interests, behaviors, location, and even retarget website visitors or previous customers. Narrow down your audience to reach those most likely to engage with your ads.

Monitor and optimize: Regularly monitor the performance of your ad campaigns and make data-driven optimizations. Track metrics such as click-through rates, conversion rates, cost per click (CPC), and return on ad spend (ROAS). Adjust your targeting, creative, and budget based on what's delivering the best results.

Test different ad formats: Experiment with different ad formats such as carousel ads, video ads, story ads, and lead generation ads. Each format has its unique benefits and may resonate differently with your audience. Testing different formats allows you to discover what works best for your brand.

Utilize retargeting: Implement retargeting campaigns to re-engage users who have previously interacted with your brand but did not convert. These campaigns can help bring back potential customers who might have been on the fence, increasing the likelihood of conversions.

Integrate with your overall strategy: Ensure your social media advertising aligns with your overall marketing strategy. Your paid ads should complement your organic content and work together to achieve your business goals. Use insights from ad campaigns to inform your organic content strategy and vice versa.

Social media advertising offers a powerful opportunity to amplify your brand's reach and achieve your marketing goals. By defining your objectives, knowing your target audience, optimizing your ad creative, utilizing targeting options, and monitoring performance, you can run effective ad campaigns that drive tangible results for your business.

Tomorrow, on Day 23, we will explore the art of storytelling on social media and how compelling narratives can captivate your audience and strengthen your brand. Get ready to craft captivating stories that leave a lasting impact!

Day 23: The Art of Storytelling on Social Media

Welcome to Day 23 of your 30-day social media growth hack journey for small business owners! Today, we'll be exploring the art of storytelling on social media and how compelling narratives can captivate your audience and strengthen your brand.

Storytelling has always been a powerful tool for communication and connection. When it comes to social media, telling stories allows you to engage your audience on a deeper level, evoke emotions, and create a memorable brand experience. Here's how you can harness the art of storytelling on social media:

Know your brand story: Start by understanding your brand's unique story—its origins, values, mission, and what sets it apart. Your brand story forms the foundation of your storytelling efforts and provides the authenticity and personality that resonates with your audience.

Define your narrative: Determine the core narrative you want to convey through your social media storytelling. This could be your brand's journey, customer success stories, behind-the-scenes glimpses, or the impact your products or services have on people's lives. Align your narrative with your brand's values and the aspirations of your target audience.

Embrace different formats: Social media offers a variety of formats for storytelling. Experiment with different formats such as long-form posts, videos, live streams, photo series, infographics, or even interactive content like polls or quizzes. Adapt your storytelling to suit the platform and capture the attention of your audience.

Create relatable characters: Introduce relatable characters in your stories, whether it's your team members, customers, or influencers. Humanize your brand by showcasing the people behind it and sharing their experiences. This

helps your audience connect emotionally and
see themselves in the stories you tell.

Evoke emotions: Emotions are a powerful tool
for storytelling. Craft stories that elicit joy,
inspiration, empathy, or nostalgia. Use visuals,
compelling language, and relatable scenarios to
evoke the desired emotions in your audience.
Emotional connections help forge deeper bonds
with your brand.

Use visuals to enhance storytelling: Visuals play
a crucial role in storytelling on social media.
Incorporate high-quality images, videos, or
graphics that support your narrative and create
a visually appealing experience for your
audience. Ensure your visuals align with your
brand's aesthetics and evoke the desired
emotions.

Keep it concise and impactful: Social media is a
fast-paced environment, so keep your
storytelling concise and impactful. Grab
attention with a compelling opening, maintain a
clear narrative arc, and deliver a memorable
conclusion. Be concise in your language,

focusing on delivering the key messages that resonate with your audience.

Encourage user-generated stories: Encourage your audience to share their own stories related to your brand. Create dedicated hashtags or campaigns that invite user-generated content. Repost and engage with the stories your audience shares, showcasing the diversity and impact of your brand.

Be consistent across platforms: Maintain a consistent storytelling approach across different social media platforms. While the specific content and format may vary, ensure your core narrative and brand values shine through. Consistency helps build brand recognition and fosters a cohesive brand experience.

Listen and engage: Pay attention to the feedback and engagement you receive from your storytelling efforts. Listen to your audience's responses, respond to comments, and engage in conversations. This builds a sense of community and reinforces the connection between your brand and its followers.

Effective storytelling on social media has the power to captivate your audience, strengthen your brand, and leave a lasting impact. By knowing your brand story, defining your narrative, embracing different formats, evoking emotions, and engaging your audience, you can create a compelling storytelling strategy that resonates with your followers.

Tomorrow, on Day 24, we will delve into the world of influencer marketing and how collaborating with influencers can boost your social media growth. Get ready to leverage the power of influencer partnerships to expand your reach and connect with new audiences!

Day 24: Leveraging Influencer Marketing for Social Media Growth

Welcome to Day 24 of your 30-day social media growth hack journey for small business owners! Today, we'll be delving into the world of influencer marketing and how collaborating with influencers can boost your social media growth.

Influencer marketing has become a popular strategy for brands to reach new audiences, build credibility, and drive engagement on social media. By partnering with influencers who have a strong following and influence in your target market, you can tap into their reach and authenticity to promote your brand. Here's how you can effectively leverage influencer marketing:

Identify relevant influencers: Start by identifying influencers who align with your brand values and target audience. Look for influencers who have a strong presence on the social media platforms your audience is active on. Consider factors such as follower count, engagement rate, content quality, and audience demographics when evaluating potential influencers.

Build relationships: Once you've identified relevant influencers, focus on building genuine relationships with them. Follow them, engage with their content, and share their posts. This helps to establish a connection and familiarity with the influencer before reaching out for collaboration opportunities.

Collaborate on content: Work with influencers to create authentic and engaging content that aligns with your brand. This could include sponsored posts, product reviews, giveaways, or influencer takeovers. Collaborate closely with influencers to ensure the content reflects your brand message while allowing them creative freedom to showcase your products or services.

Leverage their expertise: Influencers are experts in creating engaging content and connecting with their audience. Tap into their expertise and allow them to provide input on the collaboration. They understand their audience's preferences and can help tailor the content to resonate with their followers.

Track and measure performance: Set clear goals and key performance indicators (KPIs) for your influencer marketing campaigns. Track metrics such as engagement, reach, website traffic, conversions, or sales attributed to the influencer collaboration. Use tracking tools and affiliate links to accurately measure the impact of influencer-driven campaigns.

Disclosure and transparency: Ensure influencers clearly disclose their relationship with your brand in compliance with advertising guidelines. Transparency is key to maintaining trust with their audience and building credibility for your brand.

Explore different tiers of influencers: Consider working with micro-influencers as well as macro-influencers. Micro-influencers typically have a smaller following but a highly engaged audience within a specific niche. They often have more authentic connections with their followers and can provide cost-effective opportunities for collaboration.

Amplify influencer content: Once influencers have created content for your brand, amplify it across your own social media channels. Repost their content, share it in your stories, or create roundup posts featuring influencer contributions. This not only boosts the reach of the influencer content but also strengthens your brand's association with the influencer.

Nurture long-term partnerships: Building long-term relationships with influencers can be valuable for ongoing collaborations and brand advocacy. Invest in nurturing these partnerships by providing value to the influencers, engaging with their content beyond collaborations, and recognizing their contributions to your brand's growth.

Monitor and optimize: Continuously monitor the performance of your influencer marketing campaigns and optimize your strategies based on the results. Learn from each collaboration and refine your approach for future influencer partnerships.

Influencer marketing can be a powerful tool for small businesses to expand their reach, build credibility, and connect with new audiences on social media. By identifying relevant influencers, building relationships, collaborating on content, tracking performance, and nurturing long-term partnerships, you can effectively leverage influencer marketing for social media growth.

Tomorrow, on Day 25, we will explore the importance of engaging with your audience on social media and how to foster meaningful interactions that drive loyalty and growth. Get ready to take your community-building skills to the next level!

Day 25: Fostering Meaningful Engagement on Social Media

Welcome to Day 25 of your 30-day social media growth hack journey for small business owners! Today, we'll be exploring the importance of engaging with your audience on social media and how to foster meaningful interactions that drive loyalty and growth.

Engagement is a key factor in building a strong social media presence and fostering a loyal community of followers. When you actively engage with your audience, you create a sense of connection, establish trust, and encourage ongoing interaction. Here are some strategies to foster meaningful engagement on social media:

Respond to comments and messages: Make it a priority to respond to comments and messages from your audience. Acknowledge their feedback, answer their questions, and thank them for their support. Show that you value their input and are attentive to their needs.

Ask questions: Encourage conversation by asking questions in your posts and captions. Pose thought-provoking questions, seek opinions, or ask for recommendations. This prompts your audience to share their thoughts and engage with your content.

Run contests and giveaways: Organize contests or giveaways to incentivize engagement. This could involve asking users to like, comment, or share your posts for a chance to win a prize. Contests create excitement and encourage your audience to participate and interact with your brand.

Share user-generated content: Showcase content created by your audience. Repost user-generated content (with permission) and give credit to the creators. This not only acknowledges and appreciates your followers but also inspires others to engage and create content for your brand.

Use interactive features: Take advantage of interactive features offered by social media platforms. Utilize polls, quizzes, or interactive stories to encourage your audience to actively participate. These features make engagement fun and provide valuable insights about your audience.

Host live sessions: Conduct live Q&A sessions, product demonstrations, or tutorials. Live sessions allow for real-time interaction, and your audience can ask questions or provide immediate feedback. This fosters a sense of community and establishes you as an accessible expert in your field.

Participate in relevant conversations: Engage in conversations happening in your industry or niche. Comment on posts by influencers or thought leaders, join relevant hashtags, and contribute meaningful insights. This positions you as an active and knowledgeable participant in your industry.

Personalize your interactions: Take the time to personalize your responses and interactions. Address individuals by their names, acknowledge their specific comments or questions, and provide personalized recommendations or solutions. This shows that you genuinely care about your audience and their needs.

Show appreciation: Regularly express gratitude to your audience for their support and engagement. Give shoutouts to loyal followers, share testimonials or success stories, and express your appreciation for their ongoing support. This strengthens the bond between your brand and your community.

Monitor and analyze engagement: Continuously monitor and analyze your engagement metrics to gain insights into what resonates with your audience. Track likes, comments, shares, and click-through rates to understand which types of content drive the most engagement. Adjust your content strategy accordingly.

By actively engaging with your audience on social media, you create a vibrant and interactive community that supports your brand. Responding to comments, asking questions, running contests, sharing user-generated content, and personalizing interactions all contribute to fostering meaningful engagement.

Tomorrow, on Day 26, we will explore the power of partnerships and collaborations with other businesses or influencers to expand your reach and tap into new audiences. Get ready to forge strategic alliances that drive growth!

Day 26: Strategic Partnerships and Collaborations for Social Media Growth

Welcome to Day 26 of your 30-day social media growth hack journey for small business owners! Today, we'll be exploring the power of partnerships and collaborations with other businesses or influencers to expand your reach and tap into new audiences.

Strategic partnerships and collaborations can be highly effective in driving social media growth. By teaming up with complementary brands or influencers, you can leverage their existing audience and credibility to amplify your reach and connect with new potential customers. Here's how you can forge strategic alliances for social media growth:

Identify complementary brands or influencers: Look for brands or influencers whose target audience aligns with yours but are not direct competitors. Identify those with a similar brand ethos and values. For example, if you're a fitness apparel brand, partnering with a nutritionist or a fitness influencer could be a great fit.

Define the partnership goals: Clarify your goals for the partnership. Are you looking to expand your reach, drive sales, or create collaborative content? Define the mutual benefits and objectives you hope to achieve through the partnership.

Reach out and propose collaboration: Once you've identified potential partners, reach out to them with a collaboration proposal. Highlight the shared value and potential benefits of working together. Be specific about the type of collaboration you have in mind, whether it's joint content creation, cross-promotion, or co-hosting events.

Collaborate on content: Create engaging and collaborative content together. This could involve co-creating blog posts, videos, social media posts, or hosting joint live sessions or webinars. By pooling your expertise and resources, you can provide valuable content that appeals to both audiences.

Cross-promote on social media: Cross-promote each other's content on social media platforms. Share posts, stories, or videos created by your partner, and encourage them to do the same. This exposes your brand to a new audience and increases visibility.

Run joint campaigns or giveaways: Collaborate on campaigns or giveaways that offer mutual benefits. This could involve offering exclusive discounts, joint product bundles, or hosting joint contests or giveaways. By pooling your resources, you create a more enticing offer for your audience.

Leverage influencer partnerships: If partnering with influencers, collaborate on sponsored content or influencer takeovers. This allows you to tap into their influence and reach a wider audience that trusts their recommendations. Make sure the influencer's values and content align with your brand for an authentic partnership.

Track and measure performance: Set clear metrics and track the performance of your partnership efforts. Monitor engagement, reach, website traffic, or sales attributed to the collaboration. This helps you assess the effectiveness of the partnership and make informed decisions for future collaborations.

Nurture long-term relationships: Strategic partnerships can be long-lasting and beneficial for both parties. Invest in nurturing relationships with your partners. Regularly communicate, share insights, and explore new opportunities to collaborate. Long-term alliances can lead to continued growth and brand advocacy.

Evaluate and refine: Evaluate the success of your partnerships and collaborations. Assess the outcomes, learn from the experience, and refine your approach for future collaborations. Adapt your strategies based on the results and feedback to ensure continuous growth.

Strategic partnerships and collaborations offer a valuable opportunity to expand your reach, tap into new audiences, and strengthen your brand's presence on social media. By identifying complementary partners, defining goals, collaborating on content, cross-promoting, and measuring performance, you can forge alliances that drive social media growth.

Tomorrow, on Day 27, we will explore the power of social media advertising and how to leverage targeted ads to reach your ideal audience and drive conversions. Get ready to boost your social media presence through effective advertising strategies!

Day 27: Leveraging Social Media Advertising for Targeted Reach and Conversions

Welcome to Day 27 of your 30-day social media growth hack journey for small business owners! Today, we'll be exploring the power of social media advertising and how to leverage targeted ads to reach your ideal audience and drive conversions.

Social media advertising provides a powerful tool to amplify your reach, target specific demographics, and drive conversions. By strategically planning and executing ad campaigns, you can effectively reach your target audience and maximize your return on investment. Here are some strategies to leverage social media advertising for targeted reach and conversions:

Define your advertising goals: Start by clearly defining your advertising goals. Are you looking to increase brand awareness, drive website

traffic, generate leads, or boost sales?
Understanding your objectives will help you
shape your ad campaigns accordingly.

Identify your target audience: Identify your
ideal audience based on demographics,
interests, behaviors, or location. Social media
platforms offer robust targeting options,
allowing you to narrow down your audience and
ensure your ads reach the right people.

Choose the right platform: Select the social
media platform(s) that align with your target
audience and business goals. Facebook,
Instagram, Twitter, LinkedIn, and Pinterest all
offer advertising options, so choose the
platform(s) where your audience is most active.

Craft compelling ad content: Create engaging
ad content that captures attention and drives
action. Use compelling visuals, concise and
persuasive copy, and clear calls-to-action.
Tailor your messaging to resonate with your
target audience and highlight the unique value
your business offers.

Set a budget and schedule: Determine your ad budget and schedule. Allocate your budget based on your goals and the expected reach and engagement. Consider running ads continuously or during specific periods when your target audience is most active.

Utilize advanced targeting options: Take advantage of advanced targeting options offered by social media platforms. These include options like lookalike audiences (targeting people similar to your existing customers), custom audiences (targeting specific groups based on your customer data), and interest-based targeting. Utilize these options to refine your reach and maximize relevancy.

Monitor and optimize your campaigns: Continuously monitor the performance of your ad campaigns. Track metrics such as click-through rates, engagement, conversions, and return on ad spend (ROAS). Identify high-performing ads and optimize underperforming ones by adjusting targeting, ad creative, or bidding strategies.

Experiment with different ad formats: Social media platforms offer various ad formats, including image ads, video ads, carousel ads, and story ads. Experiment with different formats to determine which ones resonate best with your audience and drive the desired actions.

Implement retargeting campaigns: Retargeting allows you to reach people who have previously engaged with your brand but haven't converted. Set up retargeting campaigns to remind these potential customers of your brand and encourage them to take the next step.

Test and iterate: Test different variables in your ad campaigns, such as ad copy, visuals, calls-to-action, and targeting parameters. A/B test your ads to understand what resonates best with your audience and continually iterate to improve performance.

Social media advertising presents a powerful opportunity to reach your target audience, increase brand visibility, and drive conversions.

By defining your goals, identifying your target
audience, crafting compelling ad content,
utilizing advanced targeting options,
monitoring performance, and optimizing your
campaigns, you can effectively leverage social
media advertising for targeted reach and
conversions.

Tomorrow, on Day 28, we will explore the
importance of analyzing data and leveraging
insights to inform your social media strategy.
Get ready to unlock the power of data-driven
decision-making!

Day 28: Harnessing the Power of Data for Informed Social Media Strategy

Welcome to Day 28 of your 30-day social media growth hack journey for small business owners! Today, we'll be exploring the importance of analyzing data and leveraging insights to inform your social media strategy.

Data plays a crucial role in understanding your audience, measuring the effectiveness of your efforts, and making informed decisions to drive social media growth. By harnessing the power of data, you can optimize your content, targeting, and overall strategy. Here are some key steps to harnessing the power of data for an informed social media strategy:

Set up analytics tools: Start by setting up analytics tools such as Facebook Insights, Instagram Insights, Twitter Analytics, or third-party platforms like Google Analytics. These tools provide valuable data on reach, engagement, demographics, website traffic, and conversions.

Identify key metrics: Determine the key metrics that align with your social media goals. These could include reach, impressions, engagement rate, click-through rate, conversion rate, or average order value. Focus on metrics that directly impact your business objectives.

Analyze audience demographics: Dive into the demographic data of your social media audience. Understand their age, gender, location, interests, and behaviors. This information helps you tailor your content and targeting strategies to better resonate with your audience.

Track content performance: Analyze the performance of your content to identify trends and preferences. Measure engagement metrics such as likes, comments, shares, and click-throughs. Identify the types of content that perform well and replicate successful strategies.

Monitor referral traffic: If you have a website or blog, track referral traffic from social media platforms using tools like Google Analytics. Understand which social media channels are driving the most traffic and conversions. This insight helps you allocate resources effectively.

Utilize social listening: Implement social listening tools to monitor brand mentions, industry keywords, and customer sentiment. Listen to what people are saying about your brand and industry. This information can guide your content creation and engagement strategies.

A/B test your campaigns: Experiment with A/B testing to gather data on what works best for your audience. Test different variations of your content, including visuals, headlines, calls-to-action, or ad formats. Analyze the performance of each variant to make data-driven decisions.

Analyze competitors: Keep an eye on your competitors' social media activities. Analyze their content, engagement, and audience demographics. Identify strategies that resonate with their audience and adapt those insights to improve your own approach.

Optimize your targeting: Use data insights to refine your audience targeting. Adjust your targeting parameters based on demographics, interests, or behaviors of your most engaged and converting audience segments. This helps you reach the right people with the right message.

Regularly review and adapt: Continuously review your data and adapt your social media strategy accordingly. Identify trends, patterns, and areas for improvement. Make data-driven decisions to refine your content, targeting, and overall approach.

By harnessing the power of data, you can gain valuable insights into your audience, content performance, and overall social media strategy. Analyzing key metrics, monitoring audience demographics, tracking referral traffic, utilizing social listening, A/B testing, analyzing competitors, optimizing targeting, and regularly reviewing and adapting are crucial steps to inform your social media strategy.

Tomorrow, on Day 29, we will dive into the world of influencer marketing and explore how collaborating with influencers can boost your social media growth. Get ready to unlock the potential of influencer partnerships!

Day 29: Unlocking Social Media Growth with Influencer Marketing

Welcome to Day 29 of your 30-day social media growth hack journey for small business owners! Today, we'll be exploring the world of influencer marketing and how collaborating with influencers can boost your social media growth.

Influencer marketing has become a powerful strategy for reaching new audiences, building brand credibility, and driving engagement and conversions. By partnering with influencers who have established trust and a dedicated following, you can tap into their influence and leverage their social media presence. Here's how you can unlock social media growth through influencer marketing:

Identify relevant influencers: Start by identifying influencers who align with your brand values, target audience, and industry.

Look for influencers who have an engaged and authentic following. Consider factors such as their content quality, engagement rate, and audience demographics.

Research and vet influencers: Conduct thorough research on potential influencers. Review their social media profiles, blog posts, and previous collaborations. Check their engagement metrics, the authenticity of their followers, and their overall reputation. Ensure they have a genuine connection with their audience.

Establish goals and expectations: Clearly define your goals for the influencer partnership. Determine what you hope to achieve, whether it's increased brand awareness, driving website traffic, generating leads, or boosting sales. Communicate your expectations and discuss deliverables, timelines, and compensation.

Develop a mutually beneficial partnership: Collaborate with influencers to create content that aligns with your brand and resonates with their audience. This could involve sponsored posts, product reviews, giveaways, or guest blog posts. Ensure that the collaboration provides value to both the influencer's audience and your brand.

Leverage influencer-generated content: Encourage influencers to create authentic and engaging content featuring your products or services. This could include photos, videos, stories, or blog posts. Utilize this content across your social media channels to showcase the partnership and tap into the influencer's audience.

Amplify influencer content: Share and promote influencer-generated content on your social media platforms. Tag the influencers and provide credit. This not only increases exposure but also shows appreciation for their contribution. Encourage your audience to engage with the content and follow the influencer.

Run influencer campaigns or takeovers: Collaborate with influencers on dedicated campaigns or social media takeovers. This allows them to directly engage with your audience and provide valuable insights or experiences. It creates a sense of authenticity and builds trust among your followers.

Monitor and measure performance: Track the performance of influencer campaigns using metrics such as engagement, reach, website traffic, or conversions. Analyze the impact of the partnership on your social media growth and business objectives. Adjust your strategies based on the results.

Cultivate long-term relationships: Nurture relationships with influencers for long-term partnerships. Building a strong rapport and providing a positive experience can lead to continued collaborations. Maintain regular communication, share insights, and explore new opportunities together.

Comply with regulations and disclosure guidelines: Familiarize yourself with the regulations and disclosure guidelines surrounding influencer marketing, such as FTC guidelines in the United States. Ensure

transparency by requiring influencers to
disclose sponsored content appropriately.

Influencer marketing can be a powerful tool for
driving social media growth. By identifying
relevant influencers, conducting research,
establishing clear goals, developing a mutually
beneficial partnership, leveraging
influencer-generated content, amplifying their
content, running campaigns, monitoring
performance, nurturing relationships, and
complying with regulations, you can unlock the
potential of influencer marketing to boost your
social media growth.

Tomorrow, on Day 30, we will wrap up our
30-day journey with a recap of key takeaways
and a plan for continued social media growth.
Get ready to reflect on your progress and set
yourself up for ongoing success!

Day 30: Reflection and Continued Social Media Growth

Congratulations! You've reached Day 30, the final day of your 30-day social media growth hack journey for small business owners. Today, we'll take a moment to reflect on your progress and outline a plan for continued social media growth.

Reflecting on Your Journey:
Take some time to look back on the past 30 days and acknowledge your achievements. Consider the strategies you've implemented, the lessons you've learned, and the progress you've made. Reflect on the impact of your efforts on your social media presence, audience engagement, and overall business goals. Celebrate your wins and identify areas for improvement.

Key Takeaways:

Recall the key takeaways from your journey. Think about the strategies and tactics that worked best for your business. Consider the insights gained from analyzing data, optimizing content, engaging with your audience, and leveraging influencers. These takeaways will serve as valuable knowledge for your ongoing social media growth.

Plan for Continued Social Media Growth: Now, let's outline a plan for your continued social media growth beyond the 30-day journey. Use these steps to guide your future efforts:

Set Clear Goals: Define clear and specific social media goals aligned with your overall business objectives. Whether it's increasing brand awareness, driving website traffic, generating leads, or boosting sales, setting goals will give you a direction to work towards.

Refine Your Content Strategy: Based on the insights gained during the past 30 days, refine your content strategy. Continue creating high-quality and engaging content that resonates with your target audience. Experiment with different formats, such as videos, infographics, or live streams, to keep your content fresh and captivating.

Consistency is Key:
Maintain consistency in your social media efforts. Regularly post content and engage with your audience. Establish a content calendar and schedule your posts in advance. Consistency builds trust, encourages audience loyalty, and keeps your brand top of mind.

Continue Analyzing Data:
Continue analyzing data and monitoring key metrics to track your progress. Use analytics tools to gain insights into audience demographics, content performance, and campaign results. Adapt your strategies based on data-driven decisions to optimize your social media efforts.

Engage and Interact:
Maintain an active presence on your social media platforms by engaging with your

audience. Respond to comments, messages, and mentions promptly. Initiate conversations, ask questions, and encourage user-generated content. Building strong relationships with your audience fosters brand loyalty and advocacy.

Collaborate with Influencers:
Continue leveraging the power of influencer marketing. Identify new influencers relevant to your brand and audience. Cultivate partnerships and collaborate on campaigns that align with your goals. Influencers can help expand your reach, drive engagement, and build credibility.

Stay Up-to-Date with Trends:
Stay informed about the latest social media trends and platform updates. Social media is constantly evolving, and staying current will help you adapt your strategies to new features and user behaviors. Regularly explore new features, such as stories, reels, or live videos, to keep your content fresh and engaging.

Seek Learning Opportunities:

Invest in your own growth as a social media marketer. Attend webinars, workshops, or conferences to stay updated on industry best practices. Follow thought leaders and industry experts to gain insights and inspiration. Continuous learning will help you stay ahead of the curve.

Experiment and Innovate:
Don't be afraid to experiment and try new strategies. Social media is a dynamic landscape, and what works today may not work tomorrow. Test new ideas, analyze results, and iterate. Embrace innovation and stay open to new approaches to keep your social media efforts fresh and effective.

Monitor Competitors:
Keep an eye on your competitors' social media activities. Monitor their content, engagement strategies, and audience growth. Identify opportunities to differentiate yourself and learn from their successes and failures.

Remember, social media growth is an ongoing process that requires consistent effort, adaptation, and innovation. By setting clear goals, refining your content strategy, maintaining consistency, analyzing data, engaging with your audience, leveraging influencers, staying up-to-date with trends, seeking learning opportunities, experimenting, monitoring competitors, and continuously improving, you'll be on the path to sustained social media growth.

As you embark on your continued social media growth journey, remember the knowledge and insights you've gained during these 30 days. Adapt and refine your strategies as needed, and never stop learning and exploring new possibilities. Best of luck in your ongoing social media success!

Conclusion

Congratulations on completing your 30-day social media growth hack journey for small business owners! You've taken significant strides in enhancing your social media presence, engaging with your audience, and driving growth for your business. Throughout this journey, you've learned valuable strategies and tactics to optimize your social media efforts.

Reflecting on your progress, you've gained insights into the importance of goal setting, content optimization, audience engagement, data analysis, influencer collaborations, and staying up-to-date with industry trends. These key takeaways will serve as a solid foundation for your ongoing social media growth.

Remember that social media is a dynamic landscape, and success requires continuous learning, adaptation, and innovation. It's crucial to stay abreast of the latest trends, experiment with new strategies, and maintain a consistent presence to foster engagement and build brand loyalty.

As you move forward, keep refining your content strategy based on data-driven insights. Monitor key metrics to track your progress and make informed decisions. Cultivate relationships with influencers who align with your brand values and audience. Engage with your followers and foster a sense of community through meaningful interactions.

Furthermore, prioritize ongoing learning and professional development. Stay curious, attend industry events, and explore new tools and features to enhance your social media presence. Continuously monitor your competitors and seek inspiration from thought leaders in the field.

Most importantly, remain committed to your social media growth journey. It takes time and effort to build a strong presence, engage with your audience, and achieve your business goals. Embrace the challenges and setbacks as opportunities for growth and improvement.

Thank you for embarking on this 30-day journey with us. We hope it has equipped you with the knowledge and strategies necessary to propel your small business to new heights on social media. Remember, social media growth is an ongoing process, so keep up the momentum, stay focused, and watch your business thrive in the digital landscape. Best of luck on your continued social media success!